YAMAHA GUITAR METHOD
BOOK 1
by Will Schmid

Dr. Will Schmid is the author of the best selling *Hal Leonard Guitar Method* (in nine languages) and over forty books for guitar and banjo, cassettes, CDs, and a video tape for Hal Leonard Publishing. In addition to his own writing, Will has served as editor of a wide variety of Hal Leonard's methods and guitar publications. He is professor of music at the University of Wisconsin–Milwaukee where he chairs the Guitar Performance Program. He holds a B.A. from Luther College and a Ph.D. from the Eastman School of Music. He has given workshops throughout the United States and in Australia, Canada and Europe. From 1994-96 Dr. Schmid served as president of the 63,000-member Music Educators National Conference (MENC) and as a founder of the MENC/GAMA Guitar Task Force. Will performs as a finger-style and flat-pick guitarist in a singing duo with his wife Ann, autoharpist and director of the nationally known Stringalong Workshops.

CONTENTS

PRODUCED BY

HAL•LEONARD®
CORPORATION
7777 W. BLUEMOUND RD. P.O. BOX 13819 MILWAUKEE, WI 53213

FOREWORD

Since the first edition of this method was published in 1977, I have talked with thousands of guitar teachers about how the method worked for them. This feedback has been essential in building supplements to the method and a catalog with real integrity. When I decided to revise Book 1, I sent out a survey to a panel of leading guitar teachers, who answered a series of questions and marked up the book. In your hands is the fruit of our labors, and a further reason why the Hal Leonard Guitar Method (published in 8 languages) will gain wider acceptance by teachers and students. Thanks to Kirk Likes, Larry Beekman, Jim Skinger, Harold Hooper, Jim Cooney, John Campbell, George Widiger, Mike Alwin, John Dragonetti, Tony Collova, Gary Wolk and Debi Kossoris.

Will Schmid

YOUR GUITAR

This book is designed for use with any type of guitar — acoustic steel-string, nylon-string classic or electric. Any of these guitars can be adapted to use in a wide variety of styles of music.

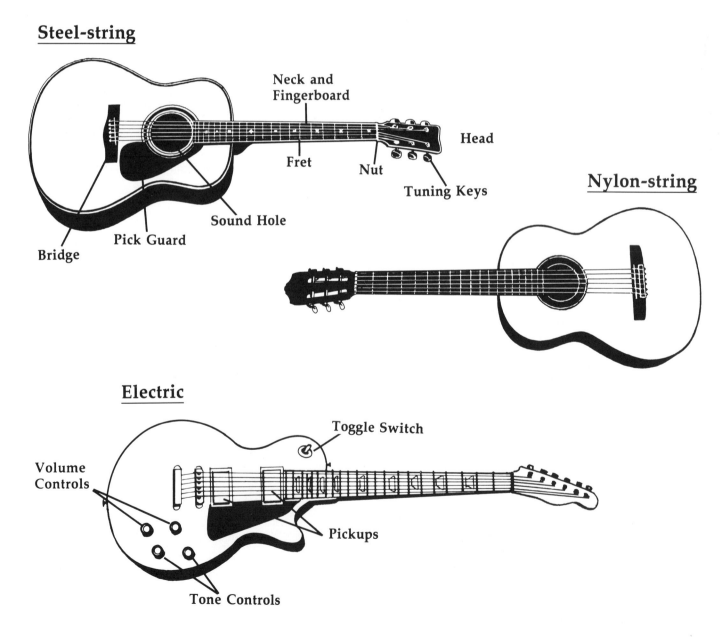

Steel-string

Neck and Fingerboard

Head

Fret

Nut

Tuning Keys

Sound Hole

Pick Guard

Bridge

Nylon-string

Electric

Toggle Switch

Volume Controls

Pickups

Tone Controls

2

TUNING ① (Indicates Audio Track Number)

TUNING KEYS

1—E
2—B
3—G
4—D
5—A
6—E

Tuning to a Piano

When you are tuning your guitar, you will adjust the pitch (highness or lowness of sound) of each string by turning the corresponding tuning key. Tightening a string raises the pitch and loosening it lowers the pitch.

The strings are numbered 1 through 6 beginning with the thinnest string, the one closest to your knee. Tune each string in sequence beginning with the **sixth** string, by playing the correct key on the piano (see diagram) and slowly turning the tuning key until the sound of the string matches the sound of the piano.

Tuning with an Electronic Guitar Tuner

An electronic tuner "reads" the pitch of a sound and tells you whether or not the pitch is correct. Until your ear is well trained in hearing pitches, this can be a much more accurate way to tune. There are many different types of tuners available, and each one will come with more detailed instructions for its use.

Keyboard

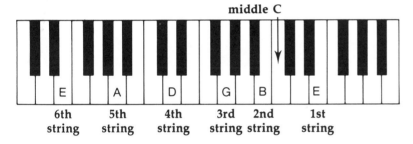

middle C

E	A	D	G	B	E
6th string	5th string	4th string	3rd string	2nd string	1st string

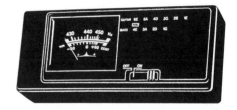

Relative Tuning

To check or correct your tuning when no pitch source is available, follow these steps:

• Assume that the sixth string is tuned correctly to E.

• Press the sixth string at the 5th fret. This is the pitch A to which you tune your open fifth string. Play the depressed sixth string and the fifth string with your thumb. When the two sounds match, you are in tune.

• Press the fifth string at the 5th fret and tune the open fourth string to it. Follow the same procedure that you did on the fifth and sixth strings.

• Press the fourth string at the 5th fret and tune the open third string to it.

• To tune the second string, press the third string at the 4th fret and tune the open second string to it.

• Press the second string at the 5th fret and tune the first string to it.

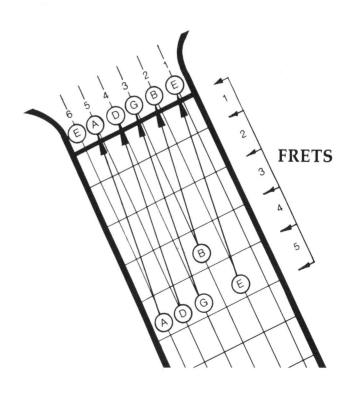

FRETS

PLAYING POSITION

There are several ways to hold the guitar comfortably. On the left is a typical seated position, and on the right is the standing position. Observe the following general guidelines in forming your playing posture:

- Position your body, arms and legs in such a way that you **avoid tension.**

- If you feel tension creeping into your playing, you probably need to reassess your position.

- Tilt the neck upwards—never down.

- Keep the body of the guitar as vertical as possible. Avoid slanting the top of the guitar so that you can see better. Balance your weight evenly from left to right. Sit straight (but not rigid).

Left-hand fingers are numbered 1 through 4. (Pianists: Note that the thumb is not number 1.) Place the thumb in back of the neck roughly opposite the 2nd finger as shown below. Avoid gripping the neck like a baseball bat with the palm touching the back of the neck.

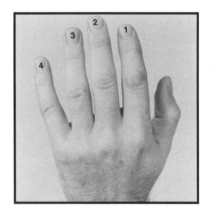

These photos show the position for holding a pick and the right-hand position in relationship to the strings. Strive for finger efficiency and relaxation in your playing.

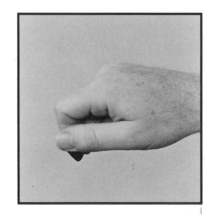
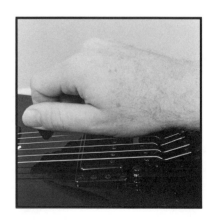

MUSICAL SYMBOLS

Music is written in **notes** on a **staff.** The staff has five lines and four spaces between the lines. Where a note is written on the staff determines its **pitch** (highness or lowness). At the beginning of the staff is a **clef sign.** Guitar music is written in the treble clef.

Each line and space of the staff has a letter name: The **lines** are, (from bottom to top) E - G - B - D - F (which you can remember as Every Guitarist Begins Doing Fine): The spaces are from bottom to top, F - A - C - E, which spells "Face."

The staff is divided into several parts by bar lines. The space between two bar lines is called a measure. To end a piece of music a double bar is placed on the staff.

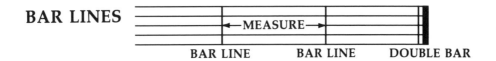

Each measure contains a group of beats. Beats are the steady pulse of music. You respond to the pulse or beat when you tap your foot.

The two numbers placed next to the clef sign are the time signature.
The top number tells you how many beats are in one measure.

FOUR BEATS PER MEASURE

QUARTER NOTE (♩) GETS ONE BEAT

The bottom number of the time signature tells you what kind of note will receive one beat.

Notes indicate the length (number of counts) of musical sound.

NOTES WHOLE NOTE = 4 beats   HALF NOTE = 2 beats   QUARTER NOTE = 1 beat

When different kinds of notes are placed on different lines or spaces, you will know the pitch of the note and how long to play the sound.

NOTES ON THE FIRST STRING

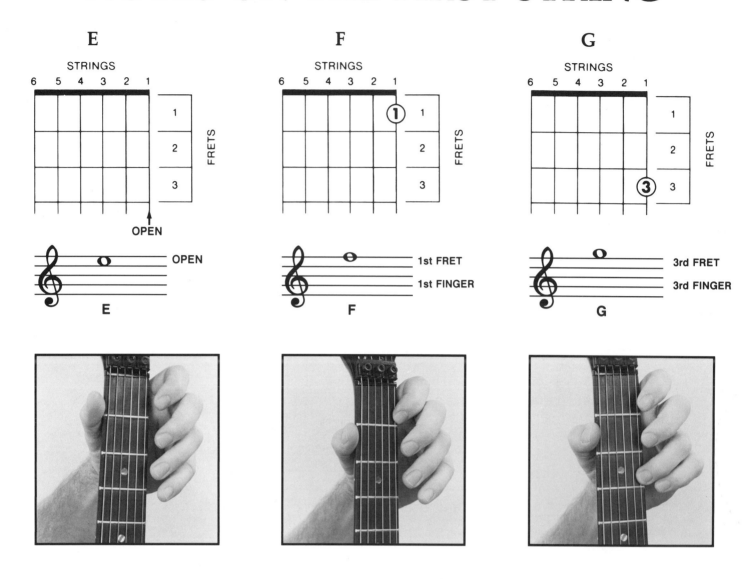

This sign (⊓) tells you to strike the string with a downward motion of the pick.

At first practice the exercises slowly and steadily. When you can play them well at a slow speed, gradually increase the tempo (speed).

Touch only the tips of the fingers on the strings.

Keep the left hand fingers arched over the strings.

Some songs are longer than one line. When you reach the end of the first line of music, continue on to the second line without stopping. Grey letters above the staff indicate chords to be played by your teacher. Measure numbers are given at the beginning of each new line of music.

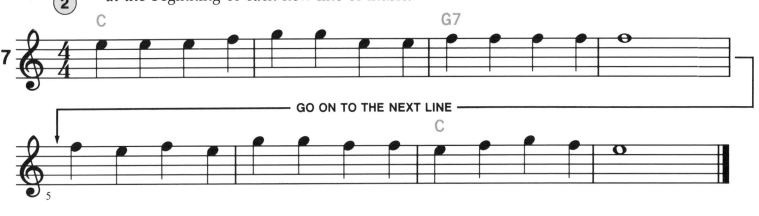

— GO ON TO THE NEXT LINE —

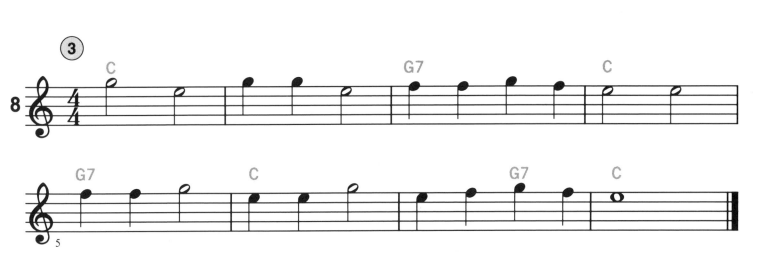

NOTES ON THE SECOND STRING

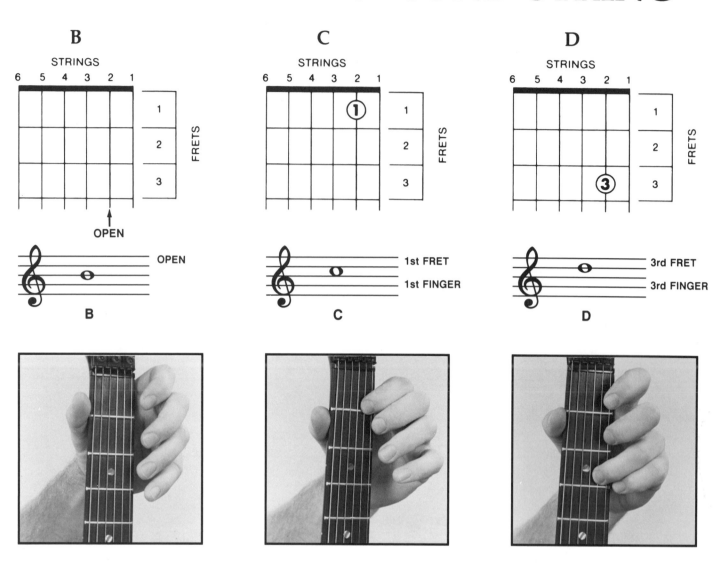

B — STRINGS — OPEN — B

C — STRINGS — 1st FRET — 1st FINGER — C

D — STRINGS — 3rd FRET — 3rd FINGER — D

9 COUNT: 1 - 2 - 3 - 4   1 - 2 - 3 - 4   Hold down 1st finger. → 1 - 2 - 3 - 4   1 - 2 - 3 - 4   1 - 2 - 3 - 4

10   1 - 2   3 - 4   1 - 2   3 - 4   1 - 2   3 - 4   1 - 2   3 - 4   1 - 2 - 3 - 4

11   1 2 3 4   1 2 3 4   1 2 3 4   1 2 3 4   1 - 2 - 3 - 4

Always practice the exercises slowly and steadily at first. After you can play them well at a slower tempo, gradually increase the speed. If some of your notes are fuzzy or unclear, move your left hand finger slightly until you get a clear sound.

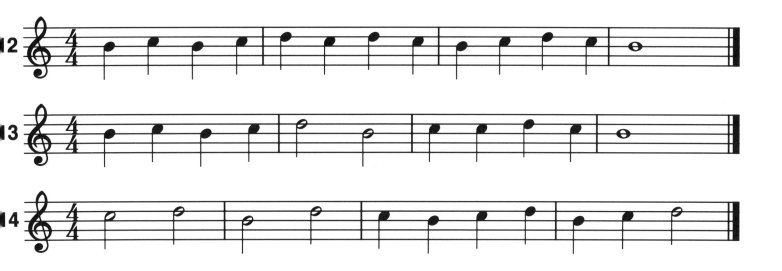

Moving From String To String

You have learned six notes now, three on the first string and three on the second string. In the following exercises you will be moving from string to string. As you are playing one note, look ahead to the next and get your fingers in position.

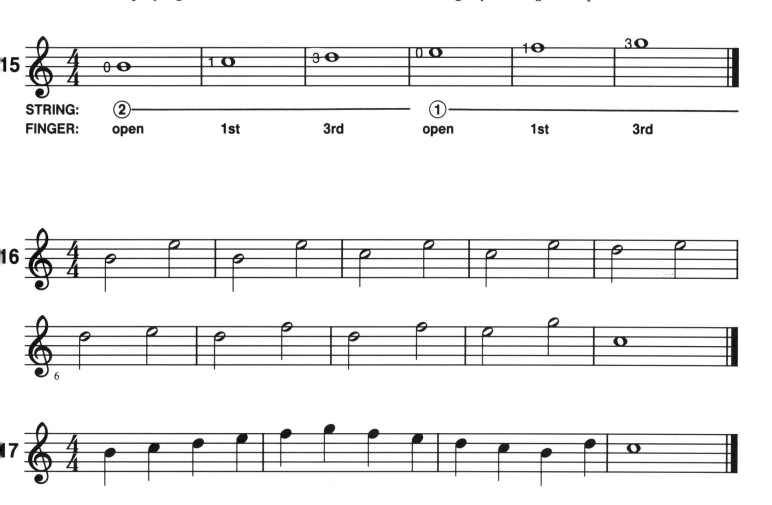

Practice these songs played on strings 1 and 2. Always begin slowly and then gradually increase the tempo. Gray chord symbols are used throughout the book to indicate that the chords should be played by the instructor.

ODE TO JOY ④ ⑤

Beethoven

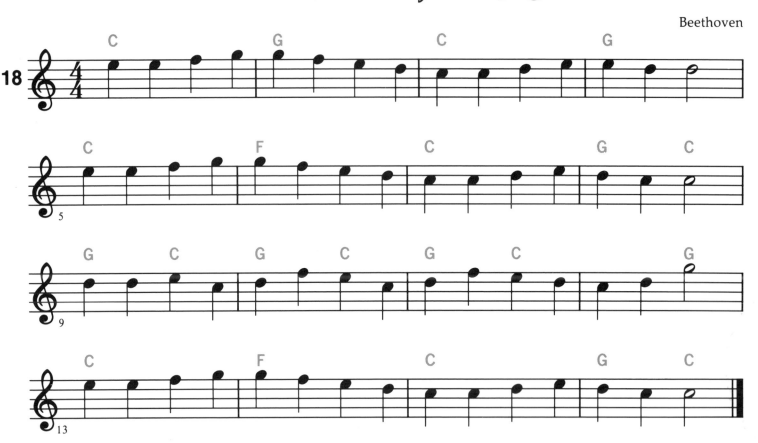

The following piece is a **round** for from 1 to 3 players. Each new player begins when the previous player gets to the asterisk (*). Play it twice through without stopping.

ROUND ⑥

NOTES ON THE THIRD STRING

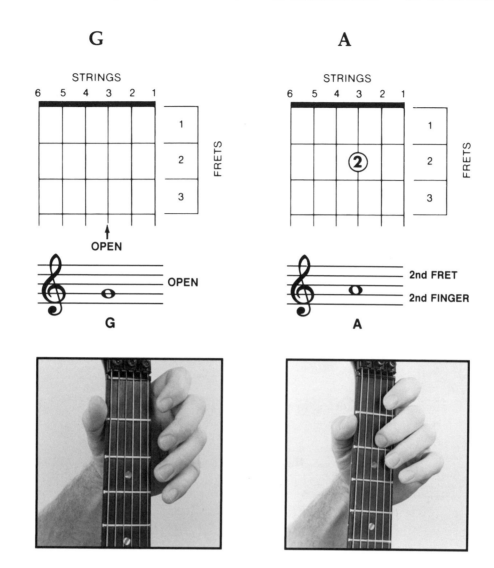

Keep the fingers arched over the strings at all times so they will be in position to finger the next note.

The following exercises and pieces use notes on strings 1, 2 and 3.

Play for accuracy; then gradually speed up. Use as a finger warm-up.

YANKEE DOODLE

A **duet** is a song that has two parts that can be played together. Practice both parts of the following duet. Ask your instructor or a friend to play the duet with you. If you have a tape recorder, you can record one of the parts and then play a duet with yourself. When you can play both parts, combine them in the optional solo below.

THE BELLS

AU CLAIR DE LA LUNE

France

AURA LEE

Some music has three beats per measure instead of four. This is indicated by the top number of the time signature. The bottom number (4) tells you that the quarter note gets one beat.

A dot after a note increases its value by one-half. In $\frac{3}{4}$ time a dotted half note (♩.) gets three beats.

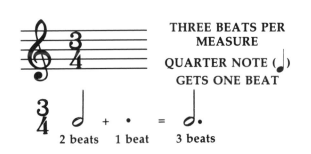

HE'S A JOLLY GOOD FELLOW 9

England

14

3-STRING CHORDS

A chord is sounded when more than one note or string is played at the same time. To begin you will be playing chords on three strings with only one finger depressed.

Strike strings 3, 2 and 1 with a downward motion. All three strings should sound as one, not separately.

C Chord

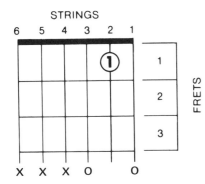

G Chord

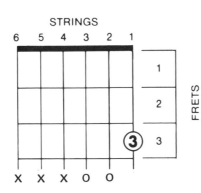

G7 Chord

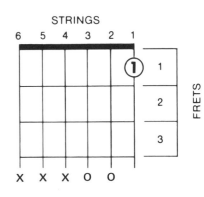

An (o) under a string indicates that the string should be played "OPEN" (not depressed by a finger).

An (x) under a string indicates that the string should not be strummed.

Keep a steady beat, and change chord fingerings quickly.

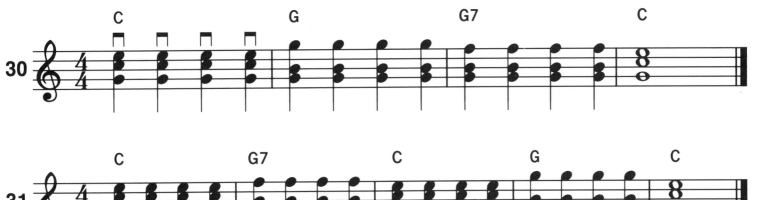

The chords above are partial chords. If you are ready to learn the full versions of these chords, turn to the **Chord Chart** on page 47.

GUITAR SOLOS

You have been playing either the melody or the chord strums in the previous exercises. Now combine the chords and the melody. First, play through the melodies (the top notes only). When you feel you know the melodies well enough, strum each chord. Finally, combine the melody and the chords. Practice the exercise slowly and steadily and gradually increase the tempo as you progress.

MARIANNE

Caribbean

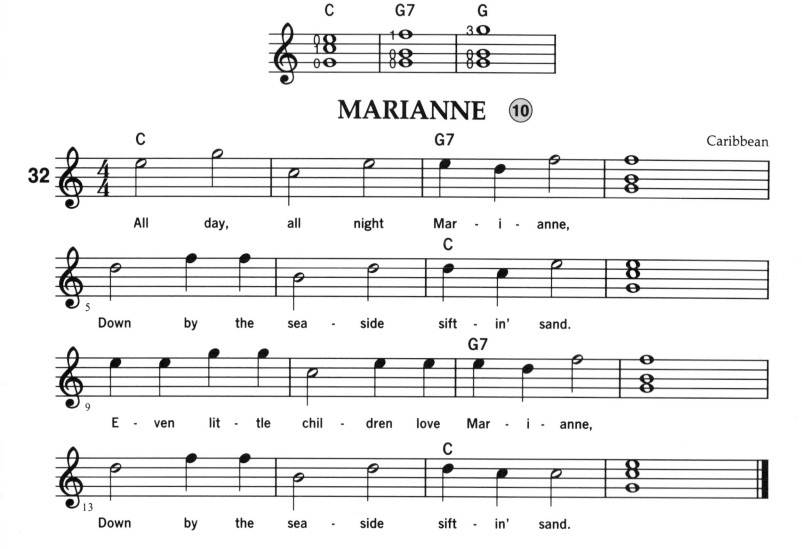

All day, all night Mar - i - anne,

Down by the sea - side sift - in' sand.

E - ven lit - tle chil - dren love Mar - i - anne,

Down by the sea - side sift - in' sand.

DOWN IN THE VALLEY

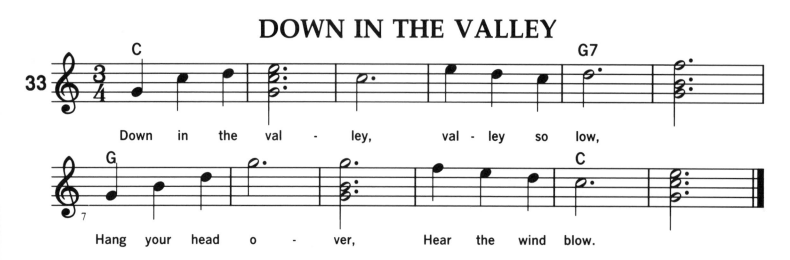

Down in the val - ley, val - ley so low,

Hang your head o - ver, Hear the wind blow.

NOTES ON THE FOURTH STRING

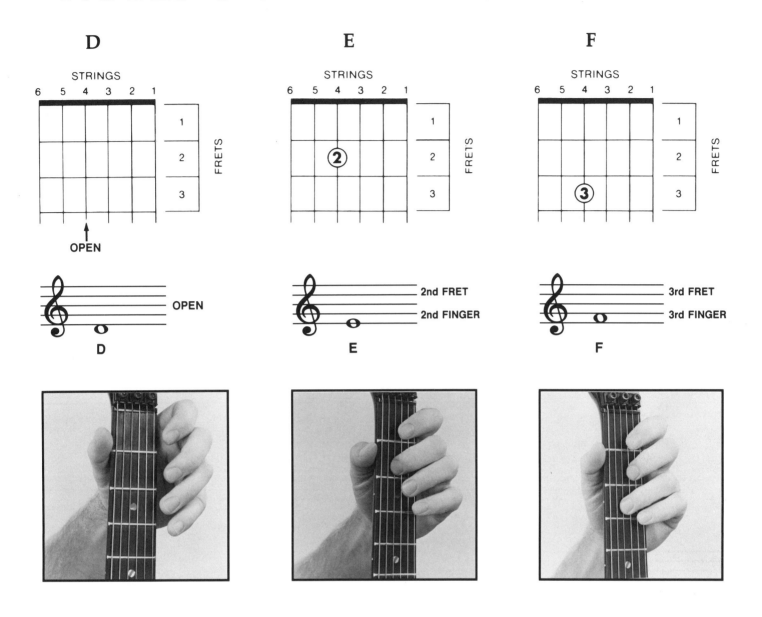

Practice each exercise carefully. Remember to keep your fingers arched over the strings.

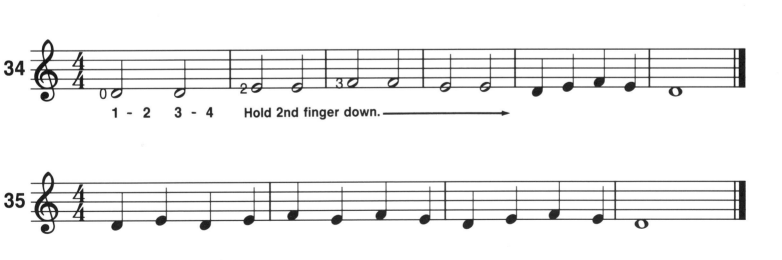

Pickup Notes

Music doesn't always begin on beat one. When you begin after beat one, the notes before the first full measure are called pickup notes. the following illustrations show several examples of pickup notes. Count the missing beats out loud before you begin playing.

THE RIDDLE SONG 11 12

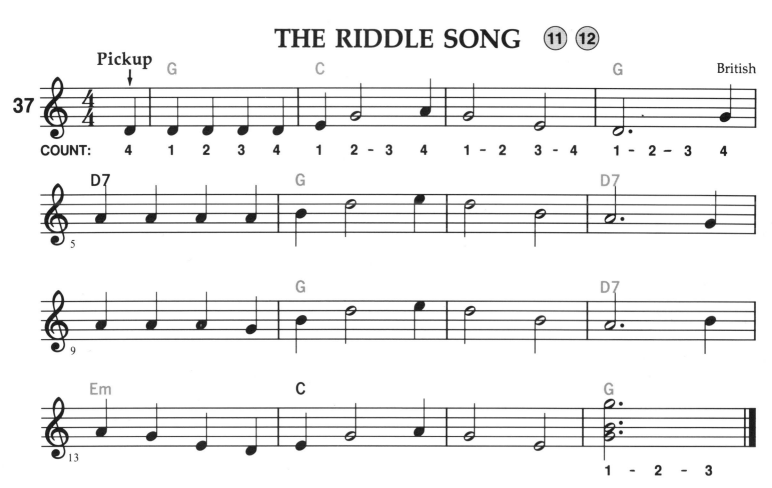

When a song begins with pickup notes, the last measure will be short the exact number of beats used as pickups.

Practice playing both the notes and then the chord strums as a duet with your teacher, a friend or a tape recorder.

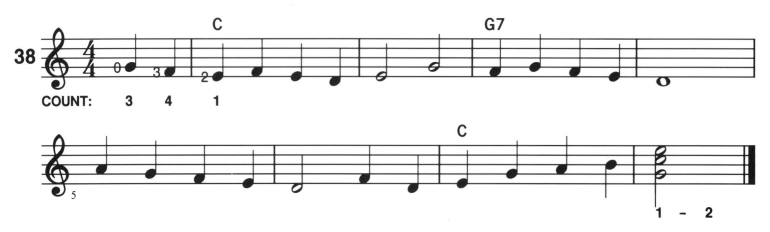

THE D7 CHORD

The D7 chord is a triangular formation of the fingers. You can play the full version of this chord right away. Arch your fingers so that the tips touch only one string each. Strum strings 4 through 1 for D7.

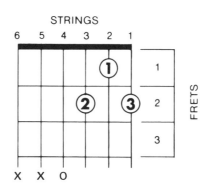

Strum once for each slash mark below.

Review the fingering for the C chord and then practice Exercise 40 until you can play it well. Whenever you are moving between the C chord and the D7 chord, keep the first finger down.

12-BAR BLUES-ROCK (13) (14)

Trade off strumming the chords and playing the melody with your teacher or a friend.

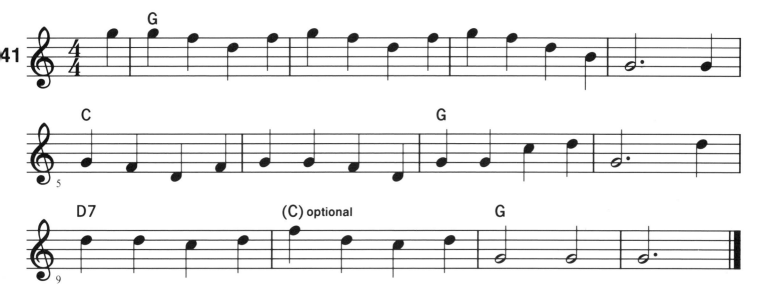

WORRIED MAN BLUES ⑮ ⑯

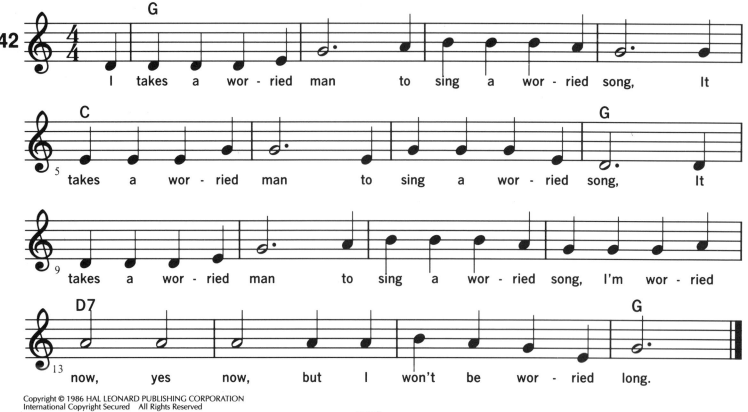

takes a wor-ried man to sing a wor-ried song, It

takes a wor-ried man to sing a wor-ried song, It

takes a wor-ried man to sing a wor-ried song, I'm wor-ried

now, yes now, but I won't be wor-ried long.

Ties

A curved line which connects two notes of the same pitch is called a tie. The first note is struck and held for the value of both notes. The second note should not be played again. Look at the following illustration of tied notes.

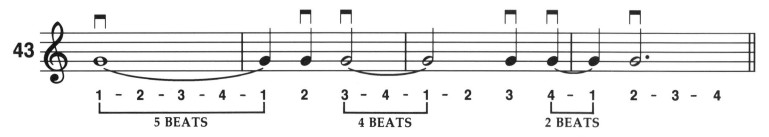

AMAZING GRACE ⑰

A - maz - ing Grace, How sweet the sound, That

saved a wretch like me; _____ I once was lost, but

now am found; Was blind, but now I see. _____

WHEN THE SAINTS GO MARCHING IN ⑱ ⑲

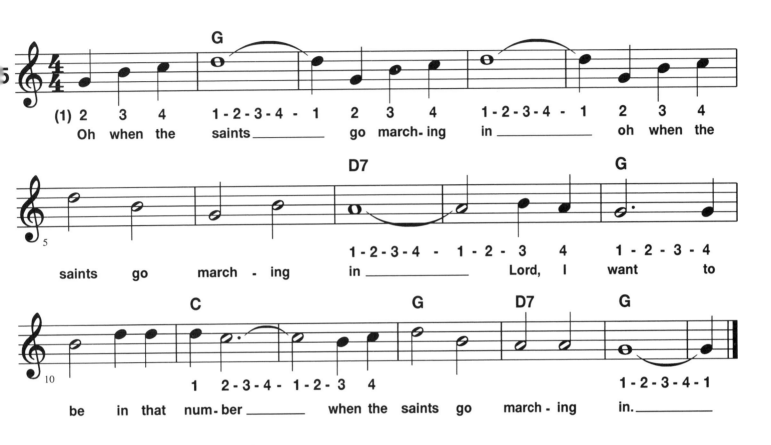

Remember that the chord letters shown in grey are to be played by your teacher.
You should play the melody only on this piece.

THE GYPSY GUITAR

NOTES ON THE FIFTH STRING

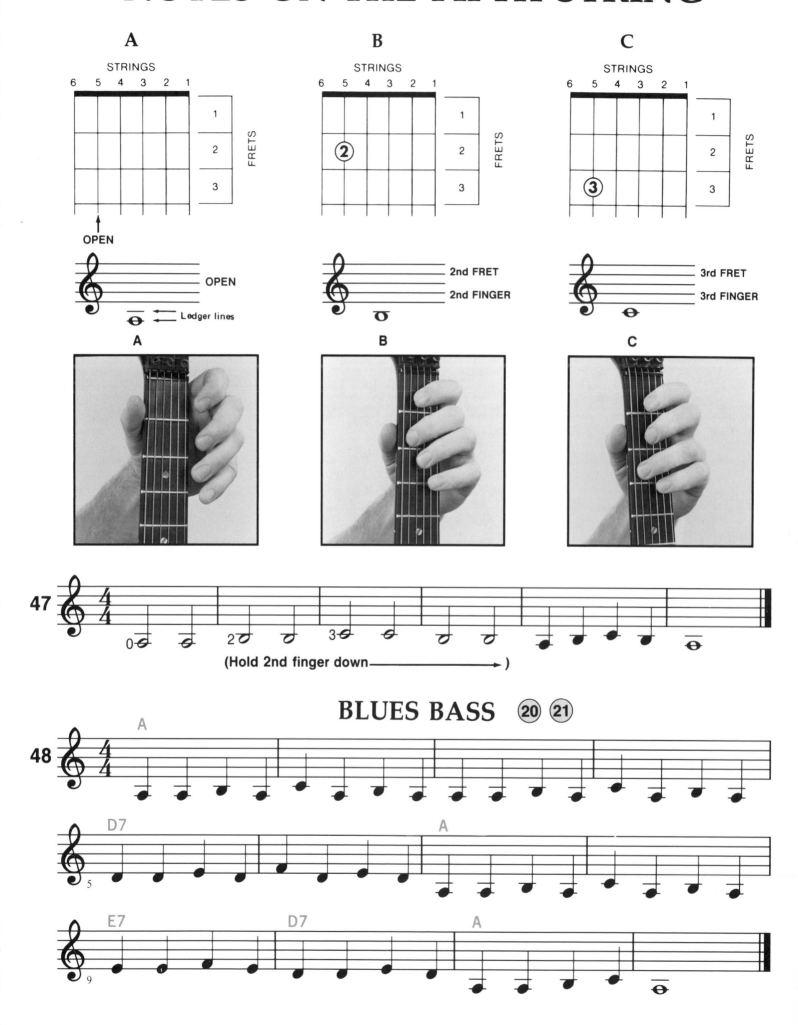

Practice these familiar melodies until you feel comfortable playing them. Remember to look ahead as you play so you can prepare for the next notes.

THE VOLGA BOATMAN

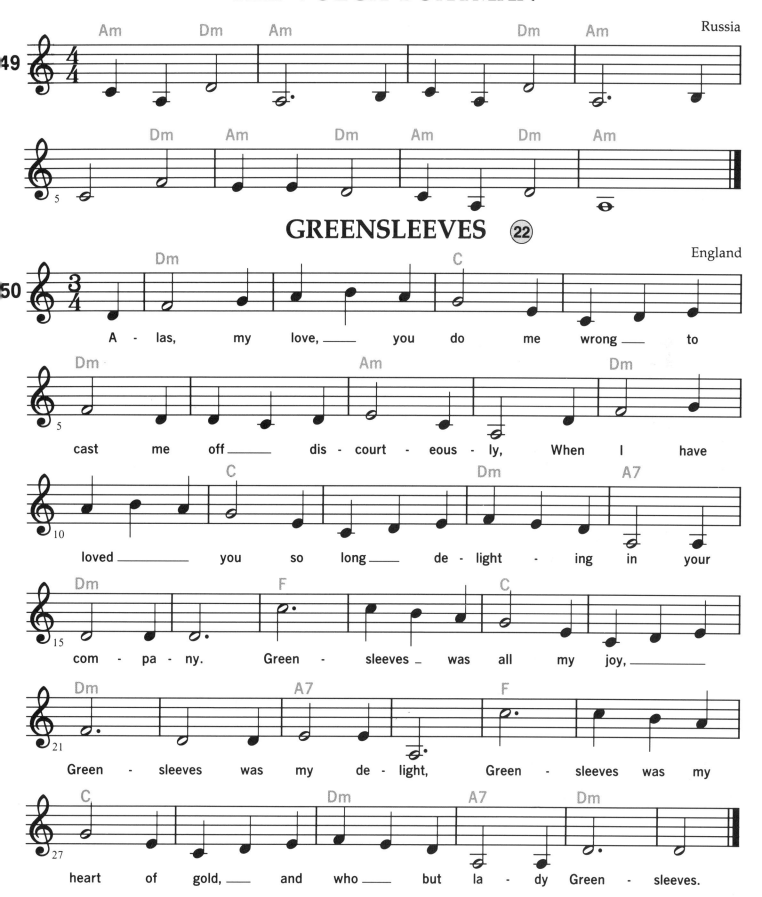

NOTES ON THE SIXTH STRING

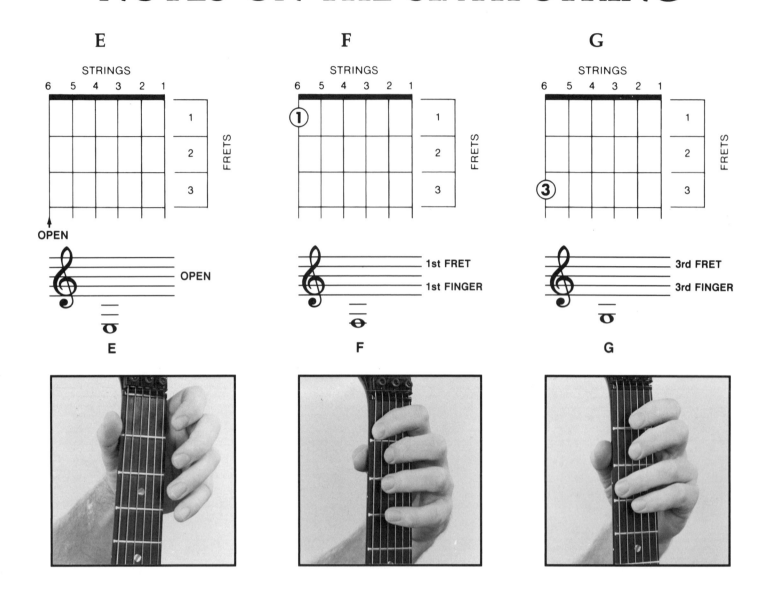

E   F   G

OPEN   1st FRET / 1st FINGER   3rd FRET / 3rd FINGER

After you play these exercises, write the letter names below each note.

Hold 1st finger down.

JOHNNY HAS GONE FOR A SOLDIER (23)

Ireland

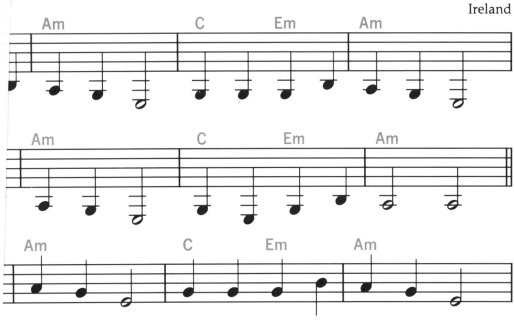

The interval between notes that have the same letter name and are eight notes apart is called an **octave**. The second half of **Johnny Has Gone for a Soldier** is written one octave higher than the first half.

Octaves

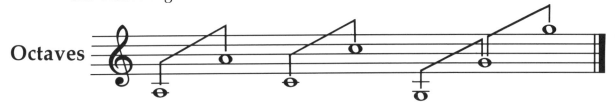

BASS ROCK

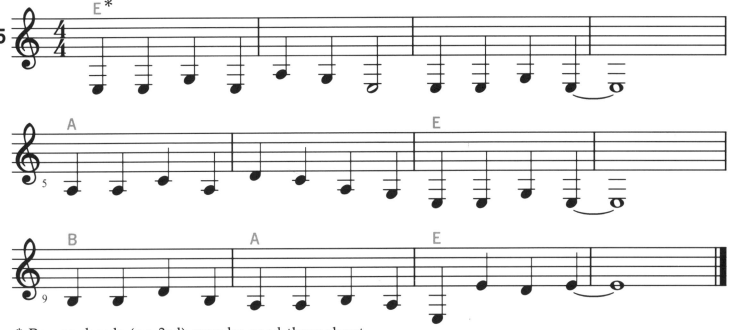

* Power chords (no 3rd) may be used throughout.

25

Half and Whole Steps

The distance between music tones is measured by half-steps and whole-steps. On your guitar the distance between one fret and the next fret is one half-step. The distance from one fret to the second fret in either direction is called a whole-step.

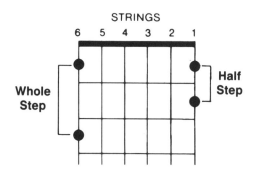

F-Sharp (F♯)

When a **sharp**(♯) is placed in front of a note, the note is raised one half-step and played one fret higher. A sharp placed before a note affects all notes on the same line or space that follow in that measure. Following are the three F♯s that appear on the fretboard to the right:

3 F♯s

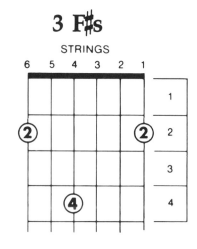

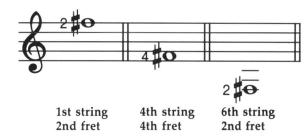

| 1st string | 4th string | 6th string |
| 2nd fret | 4th fret | 2nd fret |

Practice each of these finger exercises many times.

LONDONDERRY AIR ㉔

Ireland

26

Key Signatures

Instead of writing a sharp sign before every F in a song, one sharp is placed at the beginning of the line. This is called a key signature and indicates that every F in the song should be played as F♯. In **Shenandoah** there will be an arrow above each F♯ to remind you to play F♯.

Shenandoah is written for 1, 2 or 3 guitar parts. Part 1 (the melody) will demand that you count out the tied notes accurately. Use a metronome or tap your foot and count aloud at first. With your teacher, other friends, or a tape recorder, play part 2 and the chords.

SHENANDOAH 25

Sea Shanty

Rests

Musical **rests** are moments of silence in music. Each type of note has a matching rest which has the same name and receives the same number of counts.

Whole	Half	Quarter
4 beats	2 beats	1 beat

A rest often requires that you stop the sound of your guitar strings with your right hand as is shown in the photo to the right. This process is called **dampening** the strings. Use the edge of your right hand to touch the strings, and work for a quiet economy of motion with little unnecessary movement.

As you play the following exercises that contain both notes and rests, count aloud using **numbers for the notes** and say the word, **"Rest," for each beat of silence.**

59

COUNT: 1   2   3   Rest   1   Rest   3   Rest   Rest   2   3   4   1 - 2   Rest   Rest

The letter **R** is used in place of the word, "Rest."

60

1   2   R   R   R   2   3   4   R   R   R   R   1   R   3   4   1 - 2 - 3   R

61

1   R   R   4   1 - 2   R   R   1   2   3 - 4   1   R   R   R

In $\frac{3}{4}$ a complete measure of rest (3 counts) is written as a whole rest (▬).

62

1   2   R   1   R   R   1 - 2 - 3   R   R   R   1   R   3   1 - 2   R

ROCK 'N' REST 26

Count
rests aloud:

JACK STUART 27

Scottish

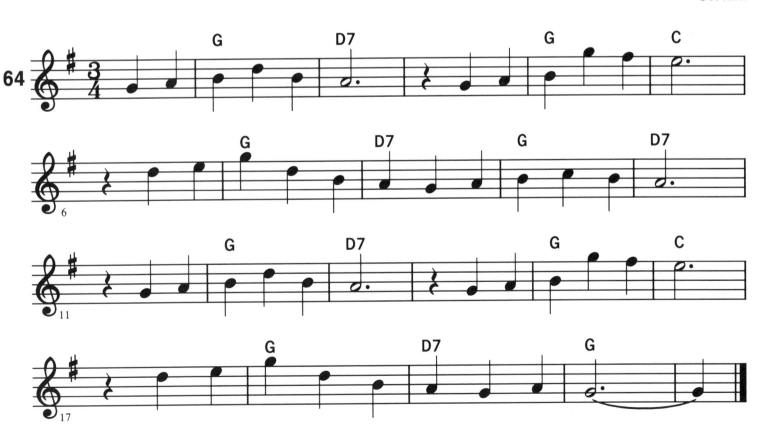

THE FULL C, G and G7 CHORDS

When you began playing the C chord and the G7 chord, you used only three strings. You can play these chords on more strings and the sound will be much fuller. Study the illustrations below for the five-string C chord and the six-string G7 chord. Place each finger in the position shown and strum the chord several times.

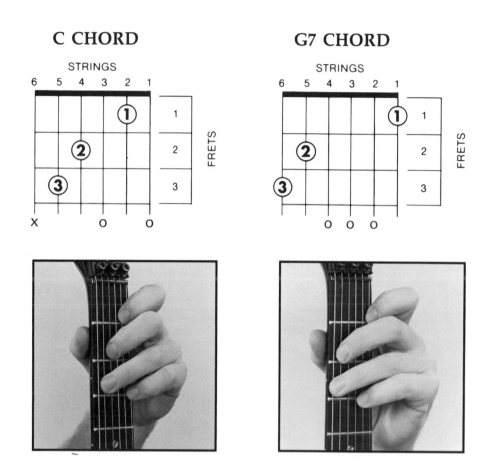

A double bar with two dots :|| is a **repeat sign**, and it tells you to play the music a second time.

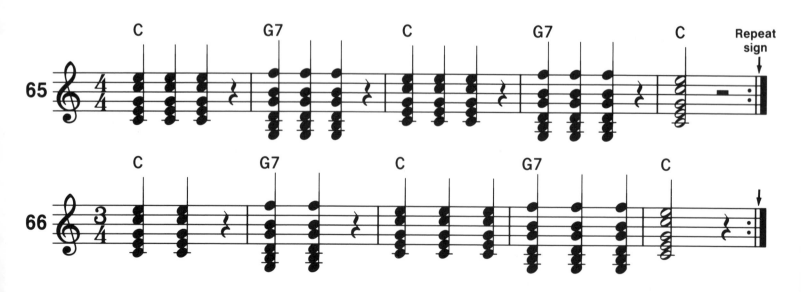

Earlier in the book you learned to play a three-string G chord. Now try the full six-string G chord for a fuller sound. Study the illustrations for the correct finger position. The formation using fingers 2, 3, and 4 will seem more difficult at first, but it will be easier to move to the C chord or the G7 chord. If your hand is small, use the formation with fingers 1, 2, and 3 or the G chord you learned earlier.

G CHORD   G CHORD

or

When you can play exercises 67 and 68 clearly and evenly, replace the rests with another strummed chord.

Practice trading off on melody and chords in these pieces.

WILL THE CIRCLE BE UNBROKEN

Country gospel

Will the cir - cle _____ be un - bro - ken, _____ by and
by, Lord, by and by? There's a
bet - ter _____ home a - wait - ing, _____ in the
sky, Lord, _____ in the _____ sky. _____

CORINNA

Blues

Oh, oh, Cor - in - na where you been so long?
Oh, oh, Cor - in - na where you been so long?
Ain't had no lov - in' since you been gone.

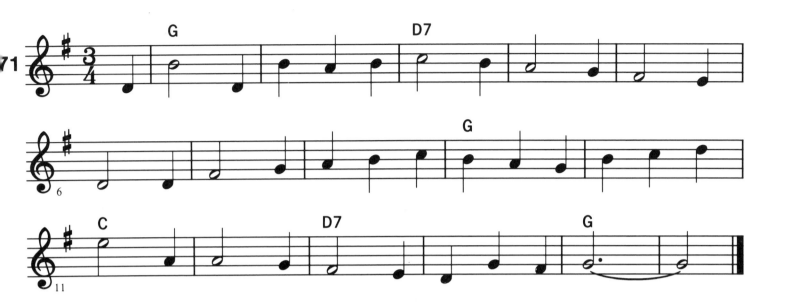

The Bass Note/Strum

When you played chords before, you strummed one chord for each beat in the measure. You can vary the strumming by alternating between a **bass note** (usually the **lowest note** of a chord and the **name** of the chord) and the **remainder of the chord**.

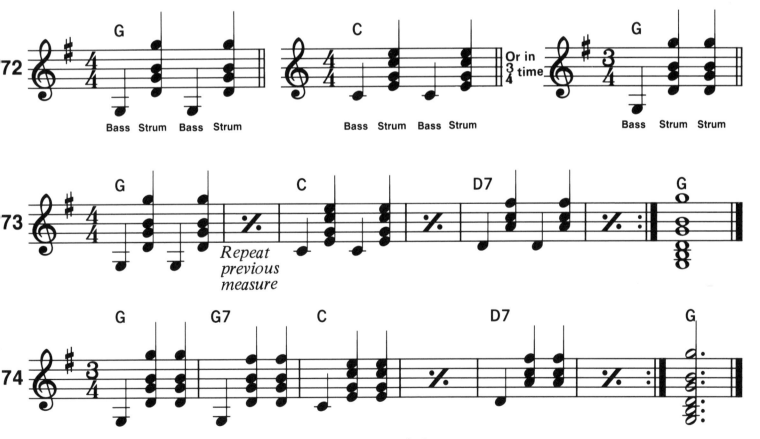

When you can play the bass-strum patterns with a steady rhythm, use them to accompany the previous songs or other songs you already know.

EIGHTH NOTES

An **eighth note** is half the length of a quarter note and gets ½ beat in $\frac{4}{4}$ or $\frac{3}{4}$.

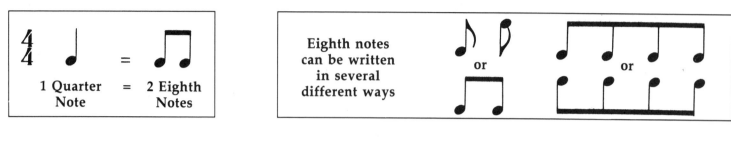

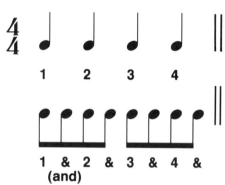

Count aloud:

Tap your foot on the beat.

Eighth notes are played with a **down (⊓) stroke** of the pick on the beat and an **up (∨) stroke** on the and (&).

Practice Exercise 76 with an alternating down and upstroke for all eighth notes and a down stroke for all quarter notes. It may help if you think that your pick is tied to your toe. When you tap your foot on the beat, the pick goes down. When your foot goes up on "and," your pick goes up.

Always practice slowly and steadily at first; then gradually increase the speed.

TIRED SAILOR

Sea Shanty

What will you do with a tir - ed sail - or? What will you do with a tir - ed sail - or?

What will you do with a tir - ed sail - or, ear - ly in the morn - ing?

FRERE JACQUES

France

Frè - re Jac - ques, frè - re Jac - ques, Dor - mez vous? dor - mez vous?
Are you sleep - ing? Are you sleep - ing? Broth - er John, Broth - er John,

Son - nez les ma - tin - es, son - nez les ma - tin - es, Din, din, don; din, din, don.
Morn - ing bells are ring - ing, Morn - ing bells are ring - ing, ding, dong, ding; ding, dong, ding.

* Frere Jacques can be played as a round. Enter when 1st player reaches the asterisk (*).

SAILORS HORNPIPE

Always check the key signature before you begin. All F's should be played F♯ in BOOGIE BASS.

BOOGIE BASS 32 33

3-PART ROUND

THE E MINOR CHORD

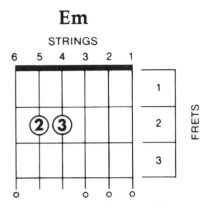

You've played the chords you learned in a variety of ways—as the full chord or only partial chords. The E minor chord can be played the same way. Study and play the example which shows the full six-string chord and a three-string partial chord.

When you are playing the E minor chord in the alternating bass note-chord pattern, use the sixth string for the bass note and the partial three-string chord. Practice the example until you can play it easily and clearly.

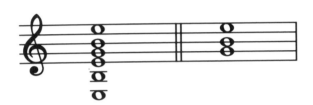

(6th string)

HEY, HO, NOBODY HOME

England

82

Hey, ho, no-bod-y home, Meat, nor drink, nor mon-ey have I none, Yet will I be mer - - - ry

SHALOM CHAVERIM

Israel

83

Sha-lom, cha-ve-rim! Sha-lom, cha-ve-rim! Sha-lom, sha-lom! Le-hit-ra-ot, le-hit-ra-ot, Sha-lom, sha-lom.

*Play as a round if you wish.

Whenever two chords have a common finger position (one or more fingers stay in the same place), you should keep the common finger on the string. In the following progression there is a common finger between the G and Em chord and a common finger between the C and D7 chord. Practice the example until you can play it steadily and without any hesitation between chord changes.

Practice trading off on the melody and chords on **Molly Molone**. When you can play the chords easily, try a bass note with two after-strums that you learned in exercise number 74.

MOLLY MALONE ㉞

Ireland

MORE ADVANCED STRUMS

The down-up stroke pattern you have already played on eighth notes can also be applied to strums. As you practice strumming the following exercises, keep your wrist relaxed and flexible. The down-up motion will be much faster and easier if you use down-up motion of the wrist only rather than of the entire arm. This wrist motion feels a little like shaking water off the hand.

BASIC DOWN-UP STRUM

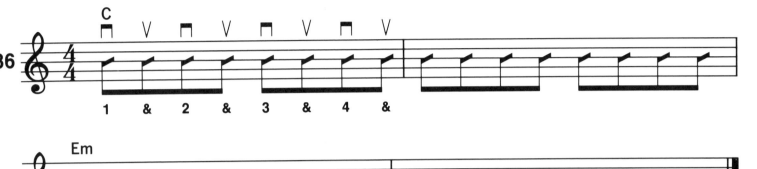

STRUM VARIATIONS

A variation of the basic down-up strum misses the upstroke or "and" of the first beat. Remember to keep the down-up motion going and miss the strings on the "and" of beat one.

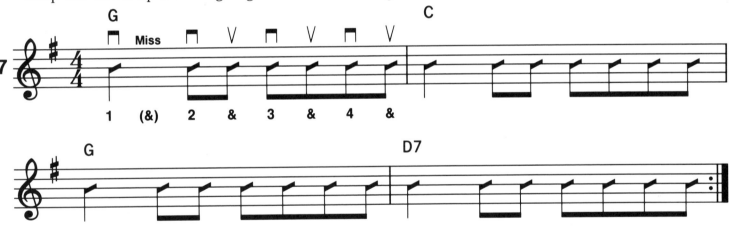

This variation misses two up strokes. Continue to strum but miss the strings on the "and" of beats one and three.

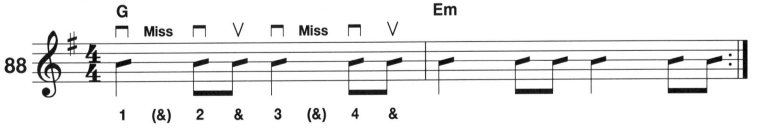

On "Simple Gifts" you can play the melody (Part 1), the harmony line (Part 2), or the chordal accompaniment.

Practice these strums before playing "Simple Gifts."

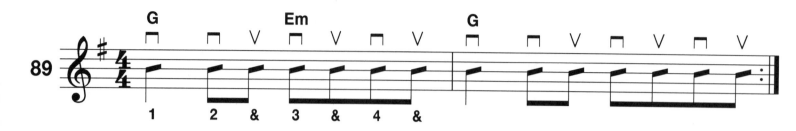

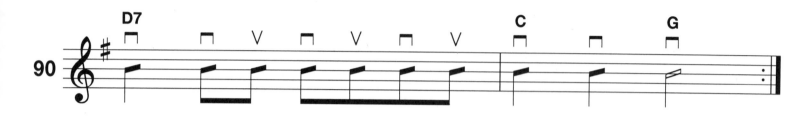

SIMPLE GIFTS ③⑤ ③⑥

Shaker song

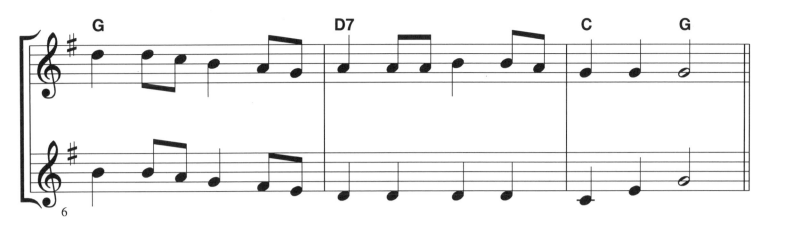
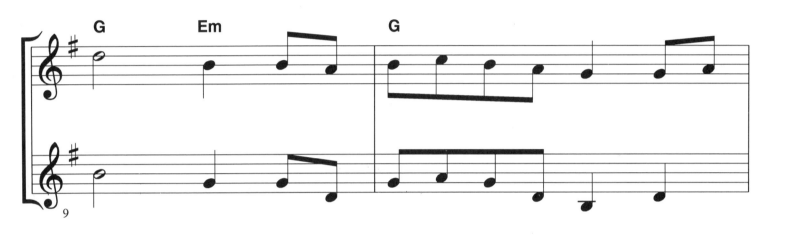
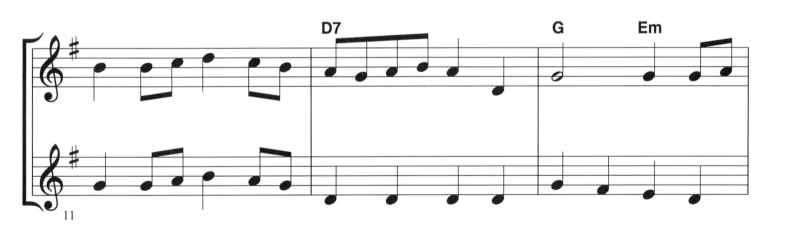
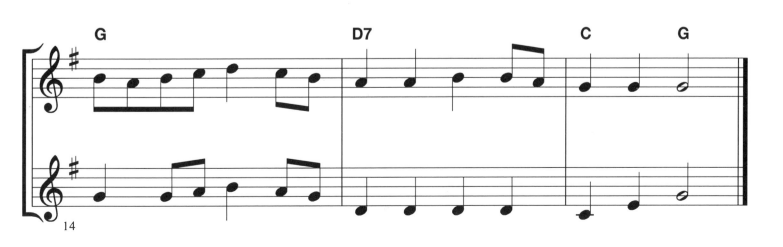

41

BASS-MELODY SOLOS

This style solo was developed on the Carter family recordings. The melody is played in the bass and long notes (𝅗𝅥 𝅗𝅥. or 𝅝) are filled in with strums. Emphasize the bass melody notes and play lightly on the strums.

ROW, ROW, ROW YOUR BOAT

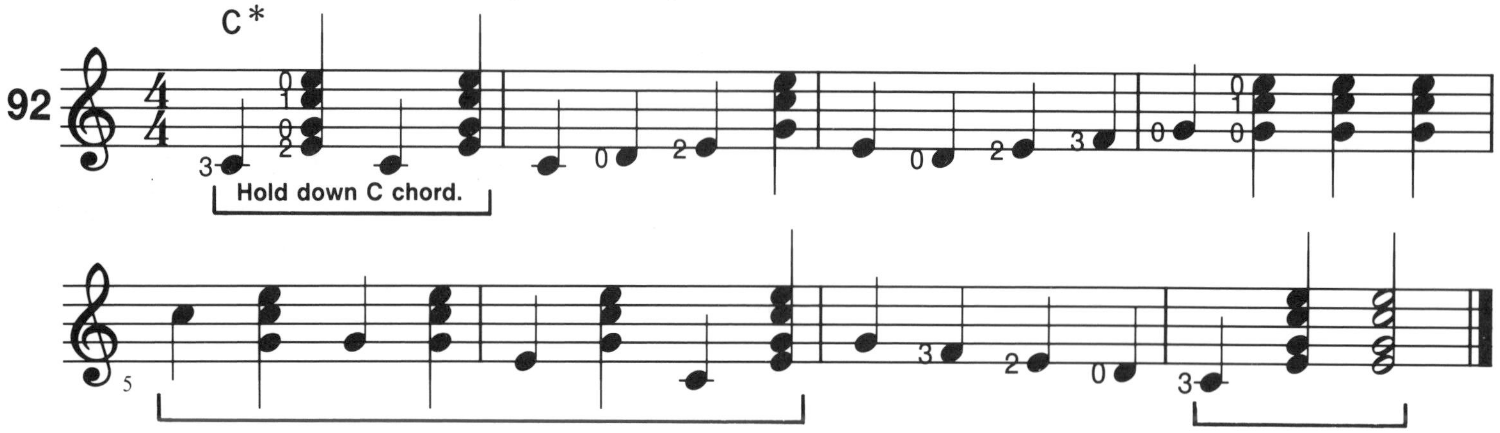
C*
92
Hold down C chord.

*You can hold your 1st finger down throughout the entire solo if you wish.

WORRIED MAN BLUES (37) (38)

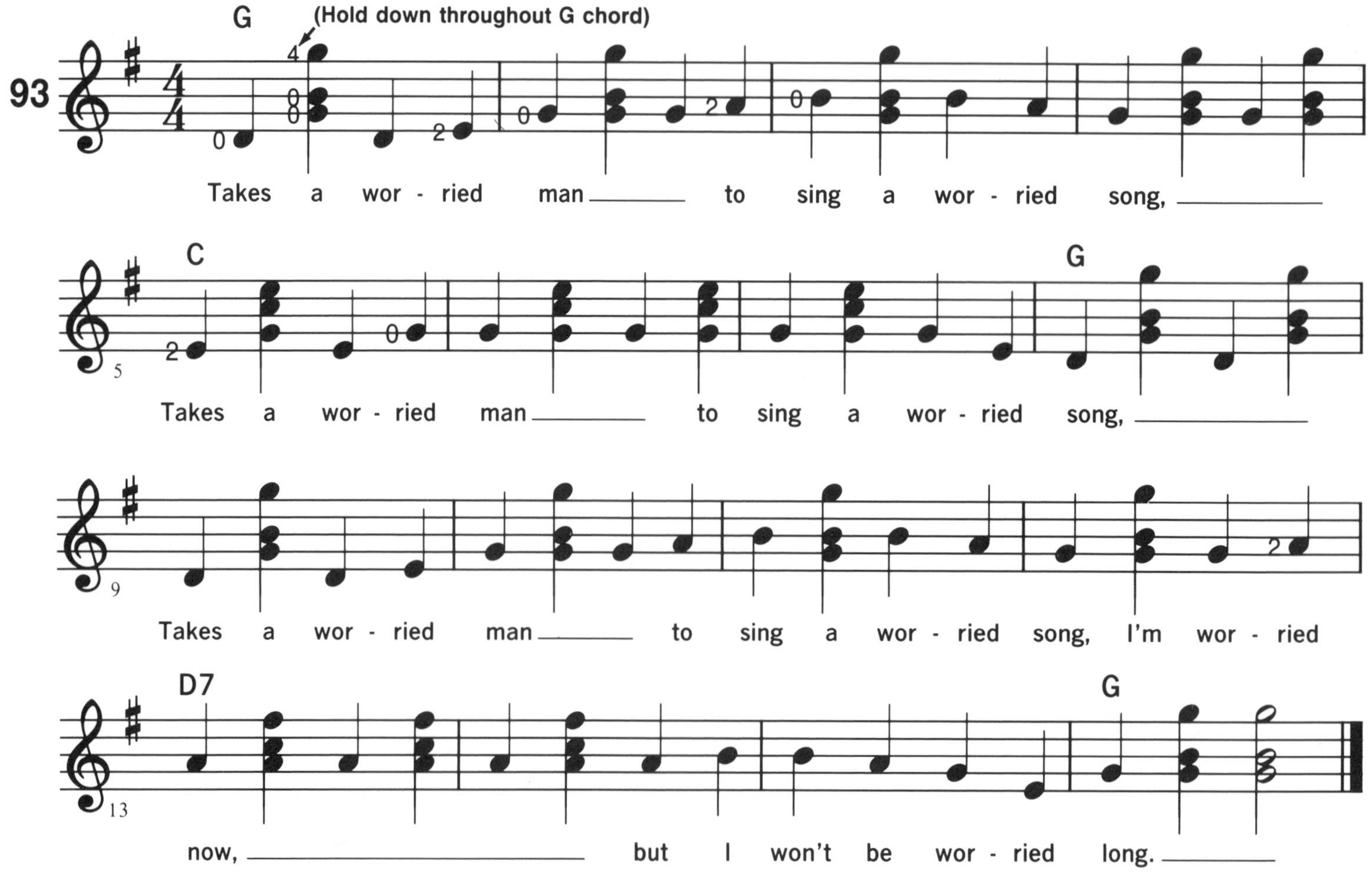
93
G
(Hold down throughout G chord)
Takes a wor - ried man ___ to sing a wor - ried song, ___
C
G
Takes a wor - ried man ___ to sing a wor - ried song, ___
Takes a wor - ried man ___ to sing a wor - ried song, I'm wor - ried
D7
G
now, ___ but I won't be wor - ried long. ___

WHEN THE SAINTS GO MARCHING IN

Oh when the saints _____ go march-ing in _____ oh when the

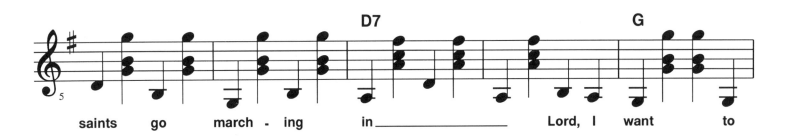

saints go march - ing in _____ Lord, I want to

be in that num-ber when the saints go march - ing in.

When you feel that these solos are coming along well, you might wish to try a variation on the strums. Instead of a single down stroke (⌐), play a down-up stroke (⌐ V). Practice this exercise; then put the down-up stroke in the solos.

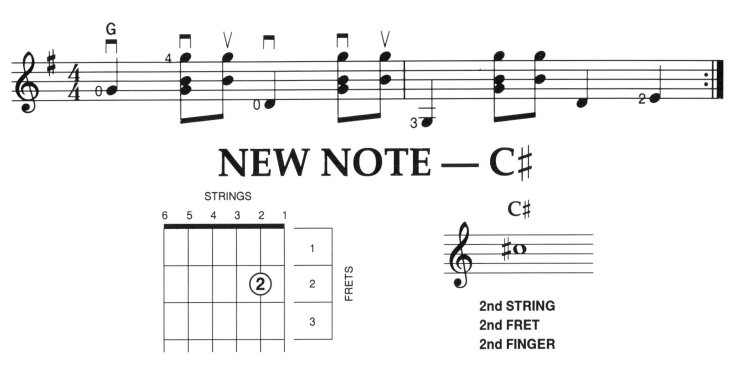

NEW NOTE — C♯

STRINGS

6 5 4 3 2 1

C♯

2nd STRING
2nd FRET
2nd FINGER

MINUET IN G

J.S. BACH
*(Guitar 2 arr.
by W. Schmid)*

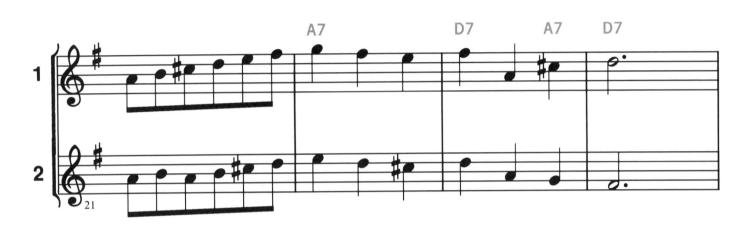

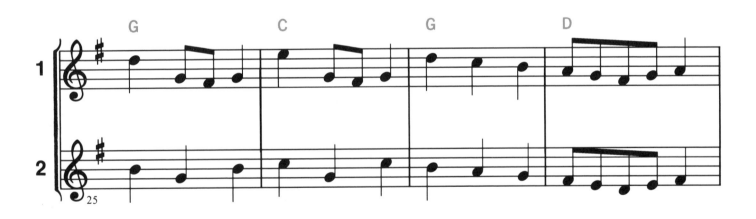

Repeat to top of page

GUITAR ENSEMBLE (41)

3-part round

After learning this Russian "Tumba" round, you may wish to play it with two or three other guitarists. Each player begins when the previous player has reached line 3 at the asterisk. A more advanced player such as your teacher may play the chords (repeating them throughout). Play the round three times through with gradually accelerating speed.

CHORD CHART

In this chart you will find the chords learned in this book as well as several other common chords you may see in music you are playing.

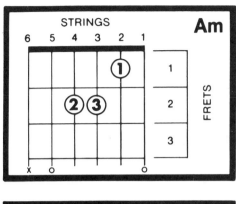
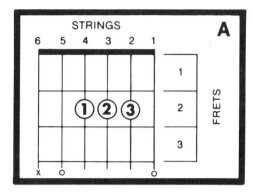
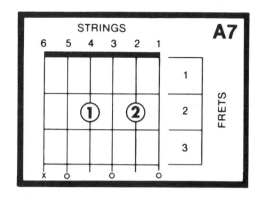

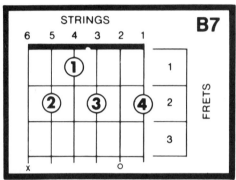
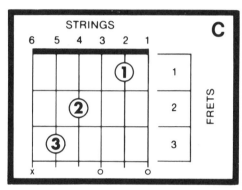
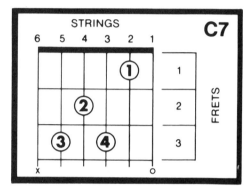

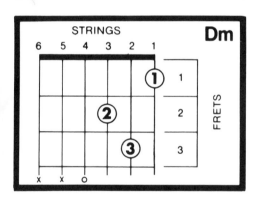
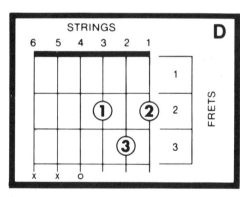
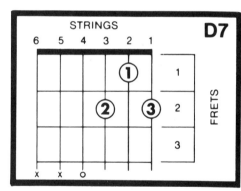

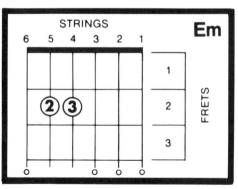
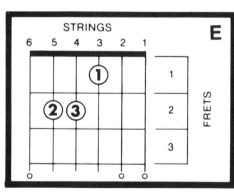
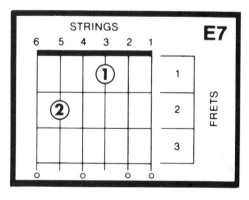

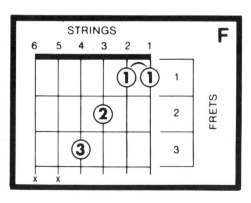
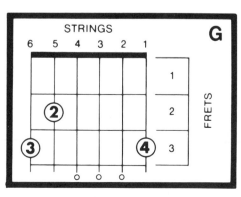
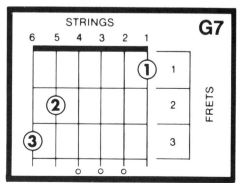

THE HAL LEONARD GUITAR METHOD

MORE THAN A METHOD ... IT'S A SYSTEM.

This comprehensive method is preferred by teachers and students alike for many reasons:

- Learning sequence is carefully paced with clear instructions that make it easy to learn.
- Popular songs increase the incentive to learn to play.
- Versatile enough to be used as self-instruction or with a teacher.
- Audio accompaniments let students have fun and sound great while practicing.

HAL LEONARD METHOD BOOK 1

Book 1 provides beginning instruction which includes tuning, 1st position melody playing (strings 1-6) the C, G, G7, D7 and Em chords, rhythms through eighth notes, solos and ensembles and strumming. Added features are a chord chart and a selection of traditional songs, including "Amazing Grace," "Greensleeves" and "When the Saints Go Marching In." The optional outstanding recording features audio demos of several exercises with various accompaniments. Tracks include acoustic and electric examples with some played at two different speeds.

00699010 Book $5.95
00699026 Book/Cassette Pack $7.95
00699027 Book/CD Pack..................................$9.95

HAL LEONARD METHOD BOOK 2

Book 2 includes studies and songs in the keys of C, G, D, Em and F, syncopations and dotted rhythms, more advanced strums, the most common 1st position chords, solos, bass runs and a variety of styles from bluegrass to blues-rock. A great selection of traditional songs including: "Simple Gifts," "Mamma Don't 'Low," "Roll in My Sweet Baby's Arms," "Jesu, Joy Of Man's Desiring," and many more. Pages are cross-referenced for supplements.

00699020 Book $5.95
00697313 Book/CD Pack..................................$9.95

HAL LEONARD METHOD BOOK 3

Book 3 includes the chromatic scale, 16th notes, playing in 2nd, 4th, 5th and 7th positions, moving chords up the neck (bar chords), finger picking, ensembles and solos, a wide variety of style studies and many excellent songs for playing and/or singing. Can be used with supplements.

00699030 Book $5.95
00697316 Book/CD Pack..................................$9.95

COMPOSITE

Books 1, 2, and 3 bound together in an easy-to-use spiral binding.
00699040 ....$14.95

GUITAR METHOD SUPPLEMENTS

Hal Leonard Pop Melody Supplements are the unique books that supplement any guitar method books 1, 2, or 3. The play-along audio features guitar on the left channel and full rhythm section on the right. Each book is filled with great pop songs that students are eager to play! Now available in book/CD packs!

EASY POP MELODIES

A unique pop supplement to any guitar method book 1. Cross-referenced with Hal Leonard Guitar Method Book 1 pages for easy student and teacher use. Featured songs: "Feelings," "Let It Be," "Every Breath You Take," "You Needed Me" and "Heartbreak Hotel."

00697281 Book..$5.95
00699148 Book/Cassette Pack $12.95
00697268 Book/CD Pack $14.95

MORE EASY POP MELODIES

A unique pop supplement to any guitar method book 2. Cross-referenced with Hal Leonard Guitar Method Book 2 pages for easy student and teacher use. Featured songs: "Long and Winding Road," "Say, Say, Say," "King of Pain," and more.

00697280 Book..$5.95
00699149 Book/Cassette Pack $12.95
00697269 Book/CD Pack $14.95

POP MELODIES PLUS

Pop supplement to Book 3. Pop Melodies Plus features "Cool Change," "Daniel," "Don't Be Cruel," "Memory," "Maneater" and many more. 14 songs in all.

00699154 Book $5.95
00697270 Book/CD Pack..................................$14.95

FOR MORE INFORMATION, SEE YOUR LOCAL MUSIC DEALER, OR WRITE TO:

HAL•LEONARD® CORPORATION
7777 W. BLUEMOUND RD. P.O. BOX 13819 MILWAUKEE, WI 53213

ROCK TRAX 1

Rock Trax is a supplement to any method book 1. It also teaches rhythm guitar, lead guitar and solo licks. The exciting play-along audio features a great-sounding rhythm section and demonstrates each exercise in the book. Rock Trax is unique because it provides the teacher with a program to teach rock guitar technique when the student begins lessons.

00699165 Book/Cassette Pack $12.95
00697271 Book/CD Pack..................................$14.95

ROCK TRAX 2

This rock guitar supplement to any method book 2 teaches rhythm guitar, lead improvisation and solo licks. The tape provides eight background rhythm tracks and demonstrates both the solo licks and new rock guitar techniques.

00697272 Book/CD Pack..................................$14.95

ROCK HITS FOR 1, 2, OR 3 GUITARS

Supplement to any method books 1 and 2. These arrangements are playable by 1, 2, or 3 guitars or class/ensemble. The audio features lead, harmony, and rhythm guitar parts with band backup on side A. Side B repeats the complete band accompaniments without guitar parts 1 or 2. "Practice notes" give the student additional playing tips. Contents: Sister Christian • Rock Around The Clock • Johnny B. Goode • Rocket Man • Sad Songs (Say So Much) • Hungry Like The Wolf • Maggie May.

00699168 Book/Cassette Pack $12.95
00697273 Book/CD Pack..................................$14.95

INCREDIBLE CHORD FINDER

A complete guide diagramming over 1,000 guitar chords in their most common voicings. The book is arranged chromatically and each chord is illustrated in three ways for three levels of difficulty: the easiest form of the chords for the beginner and the more difficult versions for the intermediate and advanced players. Note names of each string are indicated on each chord diagram to let the player know what notes are being played in the chord.

00697200 6" x 9" $4.95
00697208 9" x 12" $5.95

RHYTHM GUITAR PLAY-ALONG

Strum along with your favorite hits from The Beatles, the Rolling Stones, the Eagles, Eric Clapton, and more! The songs are presented in order of difficulty – beginning with simple three- and four-note tunes and ending with songs that contain many chords, including seventh chords and barre chords. The accompanying CD features each song recorded by a full band, so you can hear how each song sounds and then play along when you're ready. 20 songs in all: Angie • Brown Eyed Girl • Dreams • Evil Ways • Free Bird • Twist and Shout • Wild Thing • Wonderful Tonight • more. This book is intended as a supplement to the Hal Leonard Guitar Method but can also be used with any beginning guitar method:

00697309 Book/CD Pack..................................$12.95

http://www.halleonard.com
Prices, contents and availability subject to change without notice.

0200